My Poems **of View**

KIM MATTEAR

S.H.E. PUBLISHING, LLC

My Poems of View © 2021 by Kim Mattear.

All rights reserved. Printed in the United States of America. No part of this book may be used or reproduced in any manner whatsoever without written permission except in the case of brief quotations embodied in critical articles or reviews.

For information contact ;
www.shepublishingllc.com
info@shepublishingllc.com
T : 219.515.8032

Book Cover and Title Page design by Michelle Phillips of
CHELLD3 3D VISUALIZATION AND DESIGN

ISBN :
978-1-953163-25-7 (paperback)
978-1-953163-26-4 (*She*Edition)

First Edition : October 2021

10 9 8 7 6 5 4 3 2 1

I DEDICATE THIS BOOK to my late parents, Leroy and Cherryl Mattear. They both believed in me and knew my love for writing before realizing I had a gift. They would be the ones to remind me of that when they were alive. I also dedicate this book to my daughter's paternal grandmother; her name is Barbara Henderson-Thomas. She believed in me. She was my moral support when my parents died. She was not only there for my daughter but she was there for me as if I was the daughter she never had. I miss them all so much. Finally, I dedicate this book to my late nephew, Taquan "Faddy" Smith, who my family and I miss dearly. May his soul rest in heavenly peace. May all their souls rest in the Lord. Their memory will continue to live on. As much as I wish they were all here, God needed them more. In God I trust!

CONTENTS

PREFACE 1
ANOTHER DAY 1
A-B-C YOU THE BEST 3
A-B-C YOU 5
BABY BRO 7
BABIES 9
BALLER - BALLER 12
BETWEEN THE TWO 14
CHILDREN ARE THE FUTURE 16
DREAMS 19
EITHER OR 23
GENTLEMAN 27
GOOD TIMES & HAPPY DAYS 31
GUESS WHO? 34
HOW DOES IT FEEL 37
I WANT, I WANT, I WANT 41
IT GETS LONELY SOMETIME 45

IT'S GON' BE ALRIGHT	48
I WRITE	50
I'M STILL YOUNG	52
LADIES	55
LADY SINGS THE BLUES	59
LIFE'S BLUES	62
MEN	66
MOMMY DEAREST	68
MY LOVE IS YOUR LOVE	73
MY BABY DADDY	75
MY GUY	80
MY PRAYER	83
REALADY	86
POVERTY	90
SAVE THE CHILDREN	94
SEEING IS BELIEVING	98
SELF-LOVE	100
SENSITIVE	102
SO CALLED FRIEND	104
SIGNS OF LOVE	106
SLIPPING AWAY	109
THE GOOD OLE DAYS	111
THE RIGHT ATTITUDE	114

TIME FRAMES	116
WHO HAS THE POWER?	119
WHO SAID?	121
WISH I HAD OF KNOWN	123
WHO'S TO BLAME	127
WOMEN WHO LOVE TOO MUCH	130
WOMEN	134
YOU DO WHAT THAT MAN TELLS YOU TO?	137
YOU KNOW WHAT TO DO	140
ABOUT THE AUTHOR	143
ACKNOWLEDGMENTS	149
SPECIAL THANKS	152

PREFACE

THIS POETRY BOOK was not the first choice of book to release. However, it was the only book I had ready to go. I started writing two other books throughout my life, not getting very far with either of them. Constantly telling myself that I will release my book of poetry if I don't finish writing my novel beforehand. I felt the need to jump on this opportunity as soon as possible. Only the Lord knew when I'd publish my first book.

Poetry led me to the love of writing. I used to enjoy the different styles of poetry writing. I refuse to let my poetry go to the waste side. I recently sought a publishing company to possibly release my poetry during the final months of 2020 or the beginning months of 2021. I found no justification in bringing it to the light. I just continued to

MY POEMS OF VIEW

make my music. Then I was on Instagram one day, and the S.H.E. Publishing LLC's post appeared in my feed. Something about the post captured my attention to the colors black and gold, two of my favorite colors. When I learned about the details of how to get started with my book publishing, it was a wrap.

All else is history. I knew one day I'd be an author. I used to have dreams of recording music, singing and acting on stage and in movies. I always wanted to be on Broadway. I am living out my dreams, and it feels so wonderful. Most people that know me personally are aware of my passion for writing. They also know that I'm good at it. The fact that my parents always wanted to see me accomplish something that I was good at also inspired me to want to become an author one day.

At my school age, my dad used to take my written assignments to work with him, so his secretary could type them for me. He worked graveyard shift, so I'd get them the next morning. He would have so many compliments to tell me about what his co-workers, peers, and everybody had to say about me and my creative writings. They were interested in what I had to say, so they would have no problem typing anything I had written. These kinds of things always reassured me that I'm going to make my mark in this world one day. Just wishing my daughter's grandparents were able to witness it.

My mother was always encouraging me to be the best. She would enable me to utilize my gifts, reminding me they are a blessing from God that no one can take away from me. She knew I had it in me. She would call me brave and bold. She always told me that I was special and not everyone has nor possessed the gifts that I was born with. Go for it! That's precisely what I do. The confidence of the lady that raised me is all in me. Here I present to you, "My Poems of View."

MY POEMS OF VIEW

1

Another Day

Today is more than just another day.
It's another day you can do more than the day before.
Thought to pray last night or today, give thanks!

He answered one of your prayers, you woke up today.
Thankful for yesterday, today; looking forward to what tomorrow brings.

Days to come, days to pass, days ahead, days to last.
Life is what you make it! That's the difference a day makes.

MY POEMS OF VIEW

Another day lent for you to choose what becomes of you. To see today is a blessing to live in the moment and enjoy it.

The days that are given to us, need not be taken for granted or too seriously.

Another day is a blessing given and another day of living, not just another day.

It's not just what we do or what we say, it's all in how we do it, to make a way?

Making way, blessed to see another day, total blessings. Blessed to see another day, someone else missed the opportunity.

From the end of the day to the next one is not guaranteed to you nor me.

I look forward to another day to continue to be the best person that I can be.

Blessed to wake up to see another day, another day made is another day of blessings.

2

A-B-C

You the Best

A- You're so attractive
B- You're so brave.
C- You're so cuddling.
D- You're so diviner.
E- You're so extravagant.
F- You're so festive.
G- You're so grateful.
H- You're so huggable.
I- You're so inviting.
J- You're my joy.
K- You're killing me softly.
L- I could love you for life.

MY POEMS OF VIEW

M- Your love is a part of me.
N- Your love is nourishing.
O- Your love is deep like the ocean.
P- Pour your love inside of me.
Q- Your touch makes me quiver.
R- You remind me.
S- You're a smooth operator.
T- Your touch is undeniable.
U- You're unlike no other.
V- Your loves leave no vacancy.
W- Your love is warm.
X- X-ray my body.
Y- We are equally yoked
Z- Pamper me like ZSA-ZSA.

3

A-B-C You

A- You are so adorable.
B- You are so beautiful.
C- You are courageous.
D- You are so determined.
E- You are excellent.
F- You are fearless.
G- Be great.
H- Be happy.
I- You are intriguing.
J- Be joyful.
K- You are kind.
L- You are loved.
M- You are a future millionaire.
N- You are notorious.
O- Be optimistic.

MY POEMS OF VIEW

P- Be positive.
Q- You have good qualities.
R- You are a rebel.
S- You are sophisticated.
T- You are trustworthy.
U- You are unique.
V- You are victorious.
W- You are a winner.
X- You are not an X-Factor.
Y- You are the best.
Z- You are zealous.

4

Baby Bro

Baby Bro, I love you more than any words ever wrote.
I'll climb the highest mountain that's ever been climbed before.

I loved you like my seed before giving birth to my own.
You are one of the most special gifts God gave to Mom.
The last of the Mohicans, her only son.

I'm so grateful for Mommy giving birth to you.
You are a gift to me too, because I begged her to give birth to you.

Spending quality time with Dad before he went to work every night. Throughout every year you were with him catching flights.

MY POEMS OF VIEW

Mommy was so proud to be a mother to her baby boy that wouldn't let her out of his sight. So happy to see her full of pride with so much joy come out from inside.

After so many years, she did it again all in her 40's. Daddy was so happy to have you around as his little buddy.

Calling you Jake the Snake not caring for anyone else to call you any other nicknames. I couldn't believe it when I came home that night, I seen you and mom along the ambulance ride.

Born on the night of Halloween, she named you Jason, while celebrating the night. The reciprocal of thirteen, another special number to me.

I love you baby bro and all your seeds, every last three!

Kim Mattear

5

Babies

I have nothing but love for babies,
how can anyone harm them?

The most harmless beings on earth,
so full of warmth.

Unknown to the cares of
any and everything of this world.

All babies are blessings,
innocent boys and girls.

Babies are conceived by two,
they make up the future as we all do.

MY POEMS OF VIEW

The innocence they possess asked not to be here,
leaving them no choice but to depend on us.

I don't get what all the fuss is about,
besides God says "this is when we should be crying."

He knows those of a righteous and unrighteous heart,
only a lost soul would harm them.

Give them to someone who can love them,
if you don't have enough love in your heart to do so.

Babies need their feedings, readings, support,
and tender-loving-caring village.

Feeling for mommy's touch,
showered with love, feeling the strands of her hair.

With your big brown eyes that gives off a sharp stare
gazing from left to right.

Soft, smooth skin, tiny little thing,
with silky, straight, curly hair squirming around.

Whine with the cry like the purr of a cat,
purring just like one of them too.

Kim Mattear

Bundle of joy with chunky cheeks
so sweet covered in baby fat.

Full of joy, jumping, twirling,
moving and moaning as they reflex.

Stay close with a camera
to see what pose is next!

6

Baller – Baller

Baller-Baller
    Wanna be a shot caller?
        If baller, baller get shot,
            Ain't no more shot calling.

Who calling shots now?
    Baller, Baller done called
        too many shots on you
            And got you shot!

One shot at you…
    One shot at making some quick ends.
        One shot to kill your ass.
            One shot will kill you dead.

Kim Mattear

Baller, Baller
    You let him call
        too many shots!

7

Between the Two

It two sides to every story like it takes two to tango. Baby mama number one and baby mama number two.

Older than me, I'm younger than the two.
It's something he's not telling you, it's something he didn't tell me.

He spends the night with us so frequently, back and forth between the two.

He can be with you cause I'm tired of catching fits.
Getting upset with the both of you for what I'm going through!

Same two in a situation, there's just not one here to blame. Don't worry be happy together, playing with my feelings don't make it any better.

In between the both of us two, telling him to leave me alone and go be with you. He must be confused; I'm not lingering around to keep being used.

He blew my fuse, I'm sick and tired of being mentally and emotionally abused. No more wondering if he's working or somewhere else with you.

Sharing my man with another woman is one thing I just can't do. On another note, there's too many other men out here for me to choose. His involvement with me has nothing to do with you besides the truth.

MY POEMS OF VIEW

8
Children are the Future

Children of the world,
    love God who so love the world.
    Honor thy mother;
Honor thy father for your days shall be longer.

Children are the future; we should all want the best for them in every way possible. Children, praying you have parents that love you more than words can say.

Play amongst one another, be kind to one another, look out for one another. Schooling is for you to receive an education; you can think about dating later.

As the days go by, you'll be pressured by your peers, trust your heart and face your fears. Enjoy your youngin years, prevent looking back wishing you had of did that.

So darling wearing your pretty dress looking like a young beautiful Princess in your cute ponytails. No sassy talk to your parents or talking back, manners you were taught, learn them well.

Listen to your parents', respect and behave like a child should act, that's the bottom line. Pretty soon down the line, it will all make sense to you then you'll realize why.

Little girls can be so sweet and it's okay to be, no speed talk, legs closed, and watch the way you walk. Little boys stay in school, the civilized way is to follow the rules, being cool can fool you.

Keep this mental note everywhere you go, everywhere you go there will be rules. Love your friend as if he is your brother, you and your brother should be each other's protector.

Dress respectively, it's cool to hang without your trousers doing it for you. Look forward to everything in your life other than just sports, much more in store for you to explore.

Pleasure brings pain, refrain from doing bad things, negativity brings upon bad energies. Respect for girls and women, vow to never lay a hand on either of them.

I say these things to you in recognition, that you are the future of tomorrow. God is key; life is not promised; knowledge is power.

 Life can be sweet; your future is destined waiting to happen. We provide for you, here to teach you for guidance is necessary.

Enjoy your young life, be in no hurry to be grown, but don't stop growing. Before you know it, you will be grown, all off on your own.

9

Dreams

Dreams come to me like a daily breeze
that sweeps me of my feet like beating the heat.

Dreams coinciding with my visions,
so passionate about it, I love living it.

Dreams come true,
believe and make your dreams come alive.

Many dreams have crossed my mind,
big dreams all awhile from a child.

Dreams would awaken me then;
the same dreams awaken now.

MY POEMS OF VIEW

The adrenaline rollercoasting me out of my sleep
as I repeat my lines, praying not to forget.

The dialogue, the scene,
those seen in my dream all help me to remember.

Everyone should dream I suppose,
I would like to think!

Held onto my dreams from a child
refusing to ever let them go.

Knowing if I just hold onto to my dreams,
the hard work and dedication will eventually pay off.

I used to dream of being on stage rocking out every show
with a huge amount of folks in the crowd.

Thousands of people going crazy! Seemingly to be losing
their minds from the music, allegedly.

Somebody who believes in herself
and believes in her dreams.
Dreams have meanings that are just as real as the daily
energy that circulates every day.

Kim Mattear

It's all in you to make your dreams come true, all you need is you to believe in you.

Imagine your dreams coming true simply because you didn't give up on your dreams.

Let your imagination overflow allowing your vision to shine through so that you can see.

You're equipped with gifts given by The Creator who created you to be creatively enough to dream.

We are nothing without HIM! Know that your gifts glorify HIS name for HE is big, so dream BIG!

You are the only one who can see your dreams. You're the only one who can see your vision.

Happiness is found in dreams when you're in it to win it and living it, how good does it get?

Just as there will be bad days, bad dreams the same; prayerfully the good outweighs!

Dreams play a big role in the lives
of those who pay attention to them.

MY POEMS OF VIEW

Dreams are the lifeline to the spirit of our soul,
which only God and you are knowledgeable of.

Until some dreams come true some people will
look at you weird until they do.

It's obvious they don't dream enough to know or care;
your perception is different from theirs.

Life is but a dream to say the least, want to see them come
true, it's going to take a beast.

Have faith in your dreams, believe in you putting in the
work to make sure your dreams come true!

10

Either Or

Hey,
how you doing?

I pray you are in the best of health
 and in good spirits with yourself.

Hey now,
how you doing?

Your energy is normally high
filled with good vibrations.

If they don't like you for no reason,
they are just full of envy.

MY POEMS OF VIEW

People are not hard to figure out at all.

It's either one of two things,
they are either for you or they are not.

They are either with you
or they are against you.

See people need to realize
there are no in-betweens.

You're either in or out,
you're either with it or you're not.

You either got it or you don't,
you either will or you won't.

You either do or you don't,
you either did or you didn't.

There are no in-betweens,
either it is or either it isn't.

It's either a yes or no,
there's no going around it.

Kim Mattear

So, stop faking funk cause the fat lady
Sang, scoring high.

It was you acting like your shit
don't stank all along.

I can't tell you where to go,
but you got to get the hell up out of here.

11 Emotional High

My mind has gone crazy,
something is trying to tear me down.
Sparks are flying like Independence Day,
there must be a better sound.
Sitting around not knowing what to do,
thinking to myself I need you.
Help control these emotions inside,
I can no longer hide.
On the deep end of this emotional high.
my mind seems far out of my head,
something's taking over me.
I want to be free,
my emotions are now controlling me.
Emotionally drained on this emotional ride,
this rollercoaster hasn't ever gone so high!

12 Gentleman

ou were a gentleman from the moment I met you.
You are living proof that fairytales do come true.

The sweetest thing in life is you.

Good men are surely hard to find,
that's no lie.

There are still good men out here,
I have found mine.

Like Tony Braxton would say,
I love me some him!

This genuine man such a gentleman is truly the best man.

Wishing our day never ends,
while spending time with him.

MY POEMS OF VIEW

Anticipating every minute of
every second just to hear his voice.

His love is so sweet like the sweet drips of honey,
oh boy he brings me joy.

Sweet love constantly rolls off his tongue,
transmitted to my ear give me more.

You're always on my mind,
reminding me that you want to be right here.

You're the one for me and
your intentions prove it in every way.

You listen to every word I speak
often surprising me.

Catching me off guard,
oh, how attentive you are.

Loving you more,
you are the man you say you are.

Aware of my needs without me having to say a word.

Kim Mattear

I never knew a love like this exist;
it feels so good, gentlemans' can.

Am I dreaming?
I think I feel a love jones coming on strong!

Where has this gentleman been all my life,
all along?

This is the kind of love
I would vow to cherish a lifetime.

He is such a gentleman who
genuinely cares to be there.

He shows me that he cares,
how he is going to be there.

He knows exactly what to do, no talk,
allowing action to speak for itself.

Like Nike,
you just do it as a real man once said.

The qualities you possess,
it gets no better than this gentleman here.

MY POEMS OF VIEW

Your loyalty runs deep with love
overflowing all over me.

Your love is King standing tall,
alongside you stands your Queen.

13
Good Times & Happy Days

Good times are here, and happy days are here to stay! We still get to see "Good Times" that use to air on channel nine.

Remember "Happy Days" Fonzie's episode on channel five. Good times and happy days are now the new world order. The good and happy days were when you about six or seven.

Maybe even before then life was like heaven. Having fun at the park, Mom and Dad say, "be in before dark."

MY POEMS OF VIEW

It's dark now, streetlights are coming on one by one. Shoestrings tied in a twist thrown over the electric line with sneakers twirling as the wind blow.

Time to go in the house, see everybody later, let's all do it again tomorrow. In the house we go, take a bath, eat and get ready for bed.

Pajamas on, lay it down and the next minute out like a light snoring like a lion. Expecting joy to come around like she does every single morning.

Conversations of the birds and the bees taking care of business in the trees. School was cool, couldn't wait to get up and go, mama didn't raise no fool.

Rain allowed us to eat in the auditorium, huge like a forum. Playing board games all day in the classroom, now it's less work to do.

Walking home in the rain results looking all soak and wet. Cars driving through puddles splashing you every chance it gets.

Throwing off my clothes as soon as I get home, to go stand in front of the heater. Moms upset she got a ticket on her car cause time ran out on the meter.

Dad is at home in the bed getting his rest for graveyard, the night shift. Awaiting his ride every night that gives him a lift.

Trips to Magic Mountain, Knotts Berry Farm, Disneyland, even Vegas. Used to be safe to drink from water fountains, not today no way!

All the children on the block letting their parents know they want to go. Next day all the boys and girls play ding-dong ditch don't get caught.

All jokes aside, there's no show like the Huxtables from the Cosby Show, and that's law.

MY POEMS OF VIEW

14

Guess Who?

Good natured.
Good hearted.
Good peoples.
Good inside out.
Good within.
Good says God.

Sensitive, but aggressive.
Loved to be loved, but not possessive.
Far from a shit starter, more like a fire starter.
Peep game from a distance,
loud like a sports commentator.
A professional in the game,
on my way into the hall of fame.
Possess many styles,

Kim Mattear

no copycat in my swag.
Never been desperate for a man,
maybe for the man I had.
Mutual love, unconditional one,
too choosey sometimes moody.
Face carries a mean looking streak,
not mean but can be.
If you only knew what's on the inside
of those smiling cheeks so sweet.
Imperfectly shaped no bad physique,
high confidence high on self-esteem.
Honestly speaking,
God was showing out when HE made this creation.
Rhymes depicting lifestyles, writing bars along the lines.
Temperature cold,
heart is on warm,
don't make it go cold.
Always finding ways to enjoy and have fun,
will not stand for being bored.
Loner status is no determining factor for feeling alone.
Get a kick out of people,
not a kick out of talking about them.
Don't mind talking on the phone, simply love dancing,
which they don't do no more.
Sounds like I'm talking about somebody you know,
guess who?

MY POEMS OF VIEW

Steady wondering huh?
Too focused on business moves.
So as far as I'm concerned,
attracting more ways to polish my game up.
You already know who refuse to lose or ever give up on what she was born to do.

15

How Does It Feel

How does it feel when a longtime friend you trusted go around discussing your business?

How would you feel hurt and disgusted?

Listen to this though, how does it feel when you and your mother fall out like friends do?

That hurts too, doesn't it?
You wonder to yourself, is she acting like a mother?

MY POEMS OF VIEW

Am I behaving as a daughter should?
I miss my father!

How does it feel to be right and judged wrong?
Let it not destroy your confidence or your self-esteem.

How does it feel to work two weeks straight only to find out that your paycheck is short?

You'd be pissed off ready to snap, ready to take off and walk off the job, I'm sure.

How does it feel to be in love?
It feels good doesn't it, when he or she loves you back.

How does it feel to learn you and another woman is now pregnant at the same time?

Angry, hurt, heart-broken, sick to your stomach,
a painful feeling you can barely explain.

Close to the pain of another man
putting a bullet in your spine.

Understand me, for I do not wish that on anyone's life.
How else to describe pain that cuts like a knife?

Kim Mattear

No matter how it feels, you must keep it real with yourself.
Nothing in life is guaranteed, but the promises of God.

Keep in mind that, it is not always about you,
just because it involves you.

Take every day one step at a time,
make no decision off emotions.

Keep God first and He will
make all the sense out of everything.

Continue to lean on His understanding for
He will give you no more than you can bear.

Love on yourself, let nothing
or no one tear you down for no one else compares.

We fall down but we get back up,
it's called blessings not luck.

How would you feel if you knew you were in your own
way, blocking your own blessings?

If you know like I know,
count all your blessings daily.

MY POEMS OF VIEW

The wonderful feeling about life
is how we choose to deal with it, after we get hit with it.

16

I Want, I Want, I Want

All it takes is to give it all you got
to get what you want.

I want a healthy life for my daughter and I,
what does it take to get it?

Pray each day,
put in some hard work,
there's your steppingstone.

I want peace and happiness in my life,
where can I find it?

MY POEMS OF VIEW

Minding my own business, keeping a positive mind,
utilizing my time wisely.

I want a wealthy financial lifestyle;
how can I achieve it?

Work constantly and
consistently toward my goals.

Giving up is not an option, no matter what,
I tough it out.

I want a new car,
a new house,
when will I get it?

All those things are soon to come,
there's a lot to be thankful for now.

I want a respectful,
understanding,
handsome,
fun guy I can call my husband.
Is he anywhere to be found, where is he?

Kim Mattear

God knows your soulmate;
He'll send for him when
He knows you're ready.

I want my family to have more
love and respect for one another?

Will we overcome,
can we really put differences aside and
leave the past behind?

Love ourselves first,
respect each other's wishes,
compromise on that thin line.

I want the black race to stop the hate and
violence against us,
all we got is us.

Are we going to succeed?
Is it not enough blood yet that
We've shed?

There is enough love
that will frustrate the enemy
that can draw out the hate.

MY POEMS OF VIEW

There is no mountain high enough
that can shut close Heaven's gate.

There is no amount of hate that
will make me stoop low to do
what you did to me.

I want the Lord to forgive me
for my sins as
He promised all His children.

Protect me, guide me,
provide for me,
answer all my prayers.

Lord help me,
for it is not what I want,
but what you want.

As You see fit,
that shall be it,
your will is fulfilled.
For I shall get what
I deserve of all my needs.

17
It Gets Lonely
Sometime

Eyes open daydreaming
about a companion and I in our cabin.

I still want my ex,
but there's no future ever again with him.

Love won't stick around
loving somebody who doesn't love you back.

Love is not a convenience
for them only when they want it, love takes ownership!

MY POEMS OF VIEW

I'm hungry for love,
the question is: Is love hungry for me?

I am love with love all over me,
reminding me all along that I'm not alone.

Lonely only gets lonely
when one is all in their feelings.

Happiness is never lonely
because joy is there to fill the void.

We only notice when lonely is gone,
not when it's on the way home.

Only the lonely knows,
sometimes that is just the way it goes.

Pleasure and pain have found its way
just be alone, as often as needed.

Lonely hearts are dreading into darkness,
oh let there be light.

Lonely minds of the heart
are lost souls seeking its way to freedom.

Kim Mattear

Able to hear the ring desiring
to be free from self-enslavement.

Lonely is the sickness that one gets sick
and tired of dealing with.

Everybody needs love
and there's a love for everyone.

Happiness is not loneliness
although we need to be alone at times to find happiness.

Lonely cause you want to be,
or lonely cause you are still missing me?

Refrain from driving yourself
to a lonely place getting stuck there.

Lonely is misery living
with no company to invite slowly but surely dying.

Love don't love nobody,
lonely isn't lonely, cause it stays all alone on its own.

18

It's Gon' Be Alright

Don't go to sleep mad or angry,
keep a leveled head.
Make each day better than before,
as you move on to the next.
Looking to the sky, search for
and look to who we call Greater!
Wake up on the right side of the bed
for He is the Maker!
The Creator of all things,
seen and unseen.

On His understanding is where you should lean.
Give your battles to Him, you're not alone.
The battle is not yours, it's the Lord's alone.
It's going to be okay; every day is a constant fight.
Keep the faith, everything is gon' be alright.
As small as a mustard seed, He's all you need.

Kim Mattear

He has the power to change any and everything.
Choices we make brings on joy and pain.
Just as we must accept that good and bad go hand in hand.
Look forward to the future and move on from the past.
Live your life to the fullest, like everyday is your last.

Tomorrow is not promised,
joy will still come every morning.
Life goes on,
as we mourn on and soar through trials and tribulations.
After the pain,
we're back to living our normal lives again.
Almost as if it never happened,
the memories live on keeping us laughing.
Gripping my belly pacing as it's aches,
balls of cry, choking me up, gaging.
Gritting my teeth in disbelief,
what happened to being happy in the end.
It's all in the moment, make use of valueable time,
for we don't know how much of it we have to left.
Live life as if it is your last!
Don't let life live you until it ends.
No matter what may have or you may be going through.
It's gon' be alright, His promise remains true.
Who must do the other part is YOU!

19 I Write

Writing is a gift discovered as a child
allowing me to travel the mind of adventure.

It was the variety of writing styles
of poetry for me that made it worth my while.

Writing allowed me to explore
the abilities of me finding my unique side of creativity.

Thinking how neat it is
to play with words that rhyme and paint pictures.

A writer first,
the one of many gifts God showed me I had.

I write,
envisioning meanings of life's perspectives.

Writing frees me
like singing melodies, I just want to be free.

Kim Mattear

Writing in general
stimulates the brain, put it on paper.

Writing things down
will help you in any situation.

It has helped me throughout life,
writing is therapy to my soul.

Don't sweat the small stuff,
write it down you will see how small it really is.

Writing allows you to be as free
as you want to be while journaling daily activities.

Travel as far and long as you like
with whomever, whenever you like.

This is where vision meets drive
in a race of thoughts rotating like a manufacturer line.

It's the passion and excitement
for me, like a natural high when I write.

20

I'm Still Young

I'm still young,
I want to save myself,
and continue being a virgin.

Peer pressure at its best into situations of the sort.
Getting married at an early age was my last resort.
Catch a full ride straight to college after high school.
Smoking weed and drinking, yeah it seems cool.

Ditching every period each day,
not going to class, school rules!

I will not ever get good grades that will allow me to pass.
I have always heard my elders say, "If they could just do it all over again!"

Kim Mattear

I respect my elders; I pay very close attention to wisdom.
I have a life ahead of me, I will not pause it to have a baby.
I'm still young, I like participating in most school activities.

To prevent stress,
I seek out strategies.

The respect for my parents
remains even if they were to leave this earth today.

They are the only ones I can depend on
when I am down and out, hurting any kind of way.

Physically, mentally, emotionally, spiritually, and
financially, they were always there for me.

There are many opportunities for young people,
especially positive ones.

No need to rush into sex or play with guns,
you may find yourself on the run.

When intercourse does come along,
make sure wearing a condom is strictly enforced.

MY POEMS OF VIEW

It takes two to screw just because I'm a female, guys I
wouldn't put it all on you.
Do not allow knuckleheads
to mess you around like some clown.

Young world you are entitled to have fun
and make some mistakes.

Make sure through it all,
business is getting done and taken care of.

If you have not heard this until now,
you have so much potential.

Get your diploma, learn a trade,
show your credentials.

The fast life is no guarantee, it doesn't always work.
Get knowledge of the things your life is worth.

Good exist just as well as bad,
yet it does not have to be bad cause you never had.

You are still young with life ahead of you,
do not throw it away or your life is threw.

Kim Mattear

21 Ladies

Ladies, we are a blessing
to this earth like milk and honey.

Ladies, we are nurturers
and caretakers by nature.

Ladies, you deserve to be happy
with or without a man.

Ladies, uplift, enlighten,
encourage other women as such as yourself.

MY POEMS OF VIEW

Ladies, you deserve to live
in peace and harmony.

Ladies you deserve better,
bitterness is old like aged wine.

Ladies you have solidity of strength
out of this world.

Ladies you have given birth, raised,
and lead for many generations before and to come.

Ladies thank God
for the man that He has placed in your life.

Your true love is out there waiting
for you praying you're prepared for him.

Ladies, your independence
may puncture his ego at times for various reasons.

Ladies, we carry a confidence that rockets like lightning!
We love and respect our Kings.

Ladies, as strong as the guys,
of course, not physically strong like the guys.

Kim Mattear

Ladies in another sense of it,
we are generally, we are as strong them.

For we are equally yoked,
There's just some of us that's not woke nor wise.

Ladies we can be a bit much on the emotional side,
we get it guys.

Guess what?
We're only human we make mistakes all the time.

Ladies, just like we tell our children
to do it right the first time.

Ladies, it's alright
if we must do it again a second time.

Ladies, we are changing the world
like no other time ever before.

Ladies, we are in leadership,
the captain of our own ship.

Ladies, I'm so high, we are climbing mountain
hill tops, even higher and higher.

MY POEMS OF VIEW

Ladies, we are achieving,
and overachieving things only seen in dreams.

Ladies, your beauty is skin deep,
your skin tone fits you to perfection beautifully.

Ladies you are naturally beautiful
in every way you are.

Ladies, change for no one else
but for God and no one else but yourself.

Ladies, you've come too far
to stop or turn back now.

Ladies, you're never too old
to live your dreams, I am you and you are me Queen!

22

Lady Sings the Blues

Blue skies,
    blue ties.
Blue rides,
    blue tides.
Blue times,
    blue eyes.

Some days are misty, when you don't come to visit me.

I'm guilty for spilling my blues all over you.

You were there to fill in as a loved should have done.

Dealing with life's issues that I continued to hit you with.

MY POEMS OF VIEW

All awhile you and others were there to bear witness.

My family no longer had a rise after certain ones had died.

It's said that a deep-rooted-knit family is a successful one.

A friend of mines family took me into their family.

My child and I are welcome to stop by anytime.

Unfortunately, I don't feel the same about mines.

Best believe there's no love lost at the same time.

I was taught how to love and was shown what love is.

Every child, young person,
even some adults don't know a love so bliss.

It's very unfortunate for people to carry on like this.

If blue's clues only knew the lady who sing the blues.

My life is colorful filled with vanilla skies, no lie.

My life has been faced with the blues too,

Kim Mattear

I can just about bet why.
No shame, no excuses,
no escape goat, trained and thought.

Most work their way from the bottom to get to the top.

Accept what is, accept what is not, give every day,
your best shot at everything with all you've got.

The lady who sings the blues told me to make sure you do.

Be wise and do things in your life that will benefit you.

You must fool the fools that think they're fooling you.

When you lose everything,
folks' true colors come shining through.

Two times a fool, shame on you,
don't allow it to be a third time too, fool.

All I ever wanted to do is write,
sang, and entertain the blues.

I'm so glad, who knew my blues would reveal the real you!

MY POEMS OF VIEW

23

Life's Blues

The old comes along
with the new confused at times on what to do.

Everyday life hassles to be dealt with,
keeping our cool from catching fits.

It's easy to go crazy, be lazy,
or lose control, hold on to sanity.

She can be your best friend,
or your worst nightmare like on Elm Street.

Oh, don't let me get started on that wench name vanity!

Kim Mattear

No damn better than sweet faulty
found Halloween candy.

The old comes in with the new,
why you seem so confused?

We all bleed red,
one thing we all catch is the blues.

We all have played the fool,
okay and still, I refuse to be you.

I allow God to use me. Man! I refuse to be used.

Yes, we both were involved,
always remember the choice is yours.

Guns pop off and folks hit the floor,
only one way out, exit here.

Life is so beautiful at the same time it's too short.

Some may not totally agree,
that's the difference from yours.

MY POEMS OF VIEW

Brothers there are more career options
than just the world of sports.

Family not what it used to be,
who I'm going to the family reunion to see?

Bro, you know what make you family,
it's that quality-of-life name loyalty.

You either got it or you don't,
it's either you will, or you won't.

Fooling yourself with friends that's really foes.

If we're not cool to this day,
I guess we never really were.

Talking bad about me behind closed doors,
is all the confirmation I need to know.

Ignored and smiled at other
derogatory things you've said before.

Let not your heart be troubled for troubles will come.

Kim Mattear

Sustain a righteous heart with a sound mind,
powerful and positive one.

Proving points can get you locked up in the joint,
her killed, him dead, we're constantly dying.

I learned lessons being hardheaded,
hot-headed, or whatever you want to call it too!

It's only by God's grace
that I'm able to speak these words to you.

24

MEN

M- Masculine
E- Every Women Needs
N- Not a Nigga

Men, you are loved as the King you are.
Respect a Queen whether she carried you, yours, or not.
The game has been tired, trust me there's a better route.

Money isn't everything
when you're making runs with the law.

It's just a matter of time before getting caught.
Court cases and facing jail time is not it.
Hang you from a string, is the job of the prosecution team.

Kim Mattear

You are gifted with talent,
think of more positive ways to make ends meet.

It takes time with a steppingstone of one's feet.
Black man, there are still a great percentage of beautiful,
black, intelligent women all over the world.

It's not that bad,
try sticking it out with a black sister girl.

Men,
what you do is your business,
I just thought I'd donate my two cents.

To my brothermen in the pen, when you get out,
don't ever go back in.

Men our single Mother's
need you just as well as the next brother.
We should be happy to help one another.

Put down the guns for fun gung-ho!
Victory is us! Victory is won!

MY POEMS OF VIEW

Mommy,
I'd just spoken to you.
Only God knew.

                                                  I got the call
                                          Of your calling
                           and immediately started balling.

Mommy,
You had this forever young spirit
That made me think you would be around forever.

Kim Mattear

                                                             God took you
                             And Daddy at the same age
                                    But at different times.

People say
That I look like you
Now that you are not around.

                                           They used to say
                                   I looked like my Dad
                                     If looks could kill!

I get my good looks and beautiful
Smile from you,
Actually, from the both of you two.

                                                    Mommy,
                                 I see signs that tell me
                                You are still here with me.

MY POEMS OF VIEW

I know Daddy
Never
Stopped watching over me.

                                            I wasn't ready
                                  For either one of you
                                                  To go.

We know
God knows best
And takes care of the rest.

                                      I am still grateful
                                      for my brother;
                      we share a bond like no other.

Mommy,
I think if I had not left,
You would still be here.

                                You missed us so much,
                                  Not knowing how
                                        To say goodbye.

Kim Mattear

No more
Picking up the phone
To say, "hi."

                                          You were
                                          My no.1 fan.
                                        It felt like a dream.

I miss you
And all your personalities
Going off on me.

                                                      Mommy,
                               Cheryl-The-Pearl, Bouke,
                             The name Daddy gave you.

All those personalities
Got you the name
"Cherryl and them."

MY POEMS OF VIEW

                                                  You were the prettiest,
                  coolest, down-to-earth, understanding
                             Mother a child could ever have.

We
Would discuss
Any and everything.

                                                   My love is your love.
                                                     To have you back,
                                                   I would do anything.

26

My Love is Your Love

My love is your love,
from the heavens above.

My love is your love,
cause our hearts are filled with love.

My love is your love,
because it's love I have for you.

My love is your love,
because you were born into love.

My love is your love,
because your mother and father love you.

MY POEMS OF VIEW

My love is your love,
because our love made, brought us you.

My love is your love,
because I wouldn't trade you for anything in the world.

My love is your love,
because my love for you will not stop growing.

My love is your love,
no ands, ifs, or buts about the fact that I love you.

My love is your love,
there're not enough words to express it enough.

My love is your love,
I pray I'm present in your life for many years to come.

My love is your love,
you were the gift I found when I opened it.

My love is your love,
because you are loved so much.

My love is your love,
under one God is love.

Kim Mattear

27

My Baby Daddy

I thought
my baby-daddy
loved me the way I loved him.

Truth set in
what I wasn't trying to hear
from any of my friends.

A healthy and happy pregnancy is
all that mattered to me.

Loving him with my all, I wasn't the only.
Female companion,
later to become his significant other.

MY POEMS OF VIEW

When I conceived,
there was no ring to begin with.
I was in love with him, going all out on a limb.

He was my man
I thought I was the
only one pleasing him.

I thank him
for his honesty and
not informing me when I was pregnant.

On my birthday
strolling out of my teens,
wishing it was all a dream.

He had me
where he wanted me,
the whole darn time.

Not knowing if it was me, or she, he really
wanted for a while.

Knowing nothing of her,
hearing stereotypes
about me.

Kim Mattear

I was young at the time
looking at nearly
ten years my senior.

I might've been a young chic,
I carried a mature, grown,
and sexy demeanor.

Yes,
naïve and believing the story
of where he was last night always on his grind.

Believing him
even when he told me he loved me,
singing forgive me knots.

To be with this man
I refuse to compete,
my love was deep, no creep.

Plans
were in the making for them,
while my life became a trap.

MY POEMS OF VIEW

Thoughts of me
trying to trap him with a baby he asked for,
not I!

That was my man
believing everything he was saying,
shame on me.

He's still a good man
and instilled better means and good deeds
into his seeds.

Listening and believing
everything he was saying
only to find out more pipe he was laying.

The kind of pipe
that have you right for days
and cards he knew how to play.

Hey things happen,
still loved my baby daddy
until I ran into the other lady one day.

Kim Mattear

Talking about
she thought I knew of her
and what he's done for her lately.

Pregnant with their second child
I knew nothing of
conversating with all the while.

Would you believe
he planned my pregnancy,
to this very day, we are one happy family.

MY POEMS OF VIEW

28

My Guy

Tall, dark, slim with a clean cut, bald head perhaps.
Dressed to impress, in and out of uniform, so attracting.
Deep voice, outspoken with a little bit of sensitivity just for me.
Oh yes, that's him! No hard body necessary, my hunk of a man.
Knowledge of God-fearing, work oriented,
family man kind of guy.
Don't mind taking walks,
along the path, hands grasped by our fingertips in a twist.
Whispering sweet passionate wave of words
in my ear sounding like the ocean.
Reassuring me how he wants to be near when I look around,
he is always here.
Me blushing with deep thoughts of love,

Kim Mattear

with no fear.
Hugging and holding one another tight,
thinking long-term maybe a lifetime, just might.
Upholding, uplifting, not holding one another down,
constantly lifting each other up.
Free as we want to be successfully in love,
stimulating when he taps my butt like that.
A new best friend I so found in him,
so cool, he keeps me laughing.
No reason to be scared,
all treated and taken care of well.
Someone who is understanding, caring,
and forgiving, kiss me like a wishing well.
Someone who loves life and serving purpose in my life,
is my kind of guy.
Fearing nothing but the Most-High,
me-myself, and I, that's my kind of guy.
Proud to inform you who's the 1st Lady,
his love is so amazing.
He enthuses me, amuses me,
and comes with no excuses.
I love this man for taking me as I am,
loving me just for me.

MY POEMS OF VIEW

My guy is truly one of a kind,
it's hard finding them like him now.
I prayed for the right kind of guy
to be in my life now for a long time.
This time around I prayed for my lifetime partner,
I believe I found.
My guy is everything I imagined him to be
from the top his head to the bottom of his feet.
Sweet words of melody,
he's constantly thinking of me,
here with me is where he wants to be.
My KING deserves everything and
shall have whatever his wish commands.
Love and admiration fill the both of us up with no hesitation
no limitations spared.
My guy and I talk and pray of a lifetime of together,
we will make it last forever.

29

My Prayer

Dear Lord, allow me to sleep peaceful tonight.

Allow me to wake up in the morning on the right side.

Lord relieve me from all evil, harm, and weapons formed.

Lord guide me through to my dreams and goals.

Lord allow me to learn all I should know.

Lord may you send to me my daily blessings

you have waiting for me.

Lord may my good days outweigh

my bad days all of my days.

Lord allow my prayers to work and

bless you in your glorifying ways.

MY POEMS OF VIEW

I will always remember

to pray as well as praise your name.

It's the God in me, He will forever

live in me I need Him like no other.

God blesses you as well as blesses me

the absolute reason no one should envy.

Lord bring our people together in

peace and harmony without harm or strife.

Lord teach me how to deal with the pain

may I remain sane.

Lord bless my child who is smart, intellectual and bright.

Bless me Lord for you are our light, bless me to guide her right.

Bless our homes Lord as you give to us our daily bread.

Bless our paths down every road whether or not we travel it alone.

I not only pray for self, but I also pray for family, friends

as well as those unknown and unborn.

Lord bless me through all destructions,

tragedies, disasters, and catastrophic measures.

Kim Mattear

You continue to bless me with good things in life
and I can't thank you enough for it.
Lord I pray for a healthy family and loyal friends,
bless those who all I encounter.

Guide me Lord towards the healthy ways of living
as you continue to use me for the giving.
I thank you for the palm of your hands
that you have kept me in.

I thank you for my senses, my eyes, mouth, ears,
arms, hands, legs and all joined to them.
I thank you for my mobility and
the ability to do all the things for I am equipped.

I thank you for blessing me with humility and prosperity.
Lord no man, sacrifice or battle is bigger than You!
King of all Kings, I'm grateful for everything;
I thank you for choosing me.

30

REALADY

Golden girl

from the Golden State.

When it comes to her passions in life,

she doesn't play.

Talented and gifted in so many ways,

taking none of them for granted.

Utilizing every one of them,

glorifies HIS name.

Acknowledging the big fact

that she is nothing without HIM.

Kim Mattear

Excepting the things that she has the power to control,
leaving the rest all up to HIM.

Constantly in prayer about everything going on
around her known and unknown.

Realizing that she will not ever have
a bigger room larger than her room for improvement.

The r&b, rapping, acting, activist, ambassador,
music publishing, CEO chic, writer first!

So, without further a due add "author and book publisher"
under my belt as a title too.

Manifestation at its best,
the blessing came from out of nowhere.

Simply by holding onto my dreams
and not ever letting them go.

My happiness lies in them, and relies
on them, to keep *Realady* happy.

MY POEMS OF VIEW

She knows that it is not all about her,
but to serve her purpose through her gifts is all she knows.

She is here to uplift through her gifts
giving hope to those who seek it.

Peep game, it's not about the fame,
beware she's aware of how the game is played.

Born and raised to do this,
raised and brought up all around those who did it best.

Her life is more than just music,
it's more like a movie as it has always been.

Deeper than rap, new friends unnecessary,
Realady set–cutting deeper than the scissors handed to her.

Misunderstood, from the hood,
provoke me, no not good.

I wish I would, ever again, try and prove myself to man.
Choosing my battles wisely, looking forward

Kim Mattear

to no drama,

and becoming his wifey.

I'm only in competition with who I use to be,

I refuse to be anything close to phony.

I only chase after my dreams

and what God has for me.

I can only be me in which

I love so dearly, so be you.

That's the best I can do

besides pray for you.

Without a doubt I'm going to do that anyway,

in God I trust.

Remained focused on God

and goals is an absolute must.

31

Poverty

Poverty doesn't consume
 nor does it validate me.

Although it lives all around me,
I am wealthy.

I was born rich with gifts
that have the potential to change things for the good.

Poverty is a condition;
conditions are interchangeable like we as a people.

Everything is written, what if we were all the same
and had everything we ever needed?

Kim Mattear

We wouldn't search for the only One,
we truly need, who created life for us to see.

The poor has potential of becoming rich,
and the rich can potentially end up poor.

Poverty is a mindset and some of us just don't get it,
it doesn't have to be.

You have the power to change anything,
that's the power in being you.

You can do anything you put your mind to,
poverty is a mindset.

Set your mind free
and become all that you can be.

It isn't ever too late;
 you won't ever get too old to follow your dreams.

You're only as old as you feel,
if only you could get out of your feelings.

Feelings cripple folks,
then wonder why folks having strokes.

MY POEMS OF VIEW

We are better together than standing alone,
life is not a joke, stay woke.

Life has so many curve balls,
one cannot ever be so sure where it will take us.

That's exactly why it is not good to judge others,
because it can all change in an instant.

Some come from poverty
and forget where they come from.

Some are born into poverty,
that's all they know, and all it is they want.

Some come from rich homes
end up living on the streets.

Some are born into wealthiness
and are the most miserable people here on earth.

See I truly believe the ghetto is one of the
richest places there is, like Africa, rich!

Most people look at the ghetto
as a bad place when bad things happen everywhere.

Kim Mattear

Poverty is a condition
that some get accustomed to and some just refuse.

When it comes to changing your mindset,
it results to how much you care.

People make time for what they want,
easier said than done at times.

Make what you have work for you,
and work with what you have.

Think big, dream big, transforming poverty
and pain into God's creation, the Master's plan.

MY POEMS OF VIEW

32
Save the Children

One thing I will not ever understand is how can any
woman or man harm or neglect a child.

Children are the most innocent human beings
Around, ring the alarm.

Why rob them of nature's consent born into the world
Just to have a monster ruin it.

When are you coming back mommy?
Where's daddy?

I thought you loved me because you had me,
Just to leave me all alone.

Kim Mattear

Laid up and down just to have me passing
And moving all around.

No home, no family to go to,
don't know who to run to, nowhere to turn.

Who can you trust these days,
even family act like total strangers?

So full of hate, no shame for blame because a child
misbehaved, now sleep in a grave.

I rebuke you men and women who abuse and insult
children using them as prey.

There is help, there is hope,
there's a home, save a child's life today.

Do your best not to give up on your children,
no matter how bad it seems.

Deserving every bit of chance of life,
peacefully going to bed at night awakening to dawn's light.

Beware children of these bullies full of cruelty that are
filled with many insecurities.

MY POEMS OF VIEW

Hurt people, hurt other people,
I despise factual evidence which includes children.

Sick ones do it for fun or control factors
because it was done to them.

Pay attention to the patterns in your child's behavior
for it may save the both of you.

For the child's sake,
parents think to do what best for the interest of the child.

Co-parenting is necessary
just like the nine months it takes to carry.

No one parent is better than the other
when both are productively involved.

Feelings and emotions need not get the best of you
and should be set aside.

A child deserves and need all the love, care,
and concern parents should provide.

No matter how old a child grows old to be,
they will always long for a Mommy and Daddy!

Kim Mattear

Save the girls in Africa and all God's children
all over the globe.

Where are the girls in Africa, nobody cares enough?
I believe somebody knows. That, I know!

Somebody somewhere is always watching;
we can do more to save the children.

33

Seeing Is Believing

Seeing is believing, this I know, no I'm not dreaming.

Actions speaks louder than words,

don't act like you haven't heard.

It's not good to believe everything you hear or

do everything everyone else is doing.

To know is to believe in your vision only you and God can see.

That's something nobody can take away from you, but you!

Take what is inside of you and decide on the right thing to do.

Like everybody thinks to say, if they were you,

I'd do this, I'd do that.

Kim Mattear

They won't ever know until they put on your shoes.

Seeing is believing,

be very careful who you listen to.

If you can see it, you automatically believe it, right?

What about those things unseen?

Do you believe in things unknown enough

to believe in things you haven't ever seen?

To have faith,

is to believe in the unseen.

Do you believe?

34

Self-Love

They say self-love is the best love, after God I do agree.
Who else is going to love me better than me?
There are times where we are our own worst enemy!
Don't harm yourself, for you are to find someone else!

We all make mistakes,
there will be things we cannot change but must except.
Live for you and love on yourself, you're the best, you know how.
There will be some bad days, just simply give it all to God.

Self-love is not easy, it's a daily job to uphold.
Continue doing it and love yourself, loving you will overflow with a glow.
Love yourself as well as others the way you want to be loved.
Love is respect, love is kind and love is blind so open your eyes.

Kim Mattear

Self-love is rejoicing, patting yourself on the back,

like you just won a Rolls Royce.

Putting yourself first having a

positive attitude we all need to constantly rehearse.

It's not all so easy or all so hard at all, I tell you.

Lack of self-love disregard for self-respect is so selfish.

Stay out of your feelings, you can really help yourself with this small tip.

Situations can turn into life sentences behind metal bars and fences.

If we love ourselves,

we can then learn to love others.

Learn to have love for others,

the world can turn out a little better for all of us.

They say love makes the world go round,

then why not spread it all around.

I like to say God is love, and love is all we need,

like we need the leaves and the trees.

Your love is my love, I don't take abuse, no me can do!

J Lo told you love don't cost a thing, like a bird, I got wings.

You're worth much more than you know, the joy that love brings.

Self-love is a lot like His love, it's everything!

MY POEMS OF VIEW

35
Sensitive

There are many words to define me, sensitive is one of them.
Is it because I'm the baby under the astrology sign, I live?
I love hard, not a quarter, not half, but all of me I give.
Once committed, I'm dedicated and loyal from the very beginning.
This touching soul of mine is something like that of a pot of gold.
It's warm pounding with love, sweet, passionate, tender care.
Like Erykah Badu, I'm sensitive about my shit!
Excuse my French, and if I may be being a bitch...
It's that real, and sometimes that's just how it is!
Understanding is all it takes to communicate, can you relate?
Just because I'm sensitive, don't mean I live in my feelings.
I can be very forgiving because I'm very considerate of others' feelings.

Kim Mattear

Now I'm not perfect, whatsoever,

and have fallen short of this very same thing, I'm just saying.

Let's not get it twisted, there have been times

I was insensitive to some things for your information.

The difference about me,

see I immediately ask for forgiveness the moment I know I'm wrong.

My intentions are good and good intent shall remain in me always.

Karma don't know what sensitive is,

she is mean as hell and don't give a damn.

My sensitivity has a lot to do with

my creativity possessed with an overload of aggression.

As I take on the world everyday

cause it's for the taking, as I take it all in.

Coming for everything that's mine, all mines that's just it.

How many more times do I have to tell you all,

I'm sensitive about my shit!

36

So Called *Friend*

My so-called friend called me today.
Did she call you to see, how you're doing today, or to say,
"What you are doing today?"

My friend, well **my so-called friend**, came over today.
Did she come to see how you were doing,
or what you were doing?

My friend, well **my so-called friend**, wrote me a letter today.
Did she write because she's a true friend or to show and tell other's how
I responded?

Kim Mattear

My friend, well **my so-called friend**, picked me up for lunch today.
Did she invite me out for the fun of it,
or to make fun out of me?

My friend, **well my so-called friend**, told me I should leave my man.
Did she say that because it's true, or because she wants him or he wants her too?

My friend, well **my so-called friend**,
told me I was the only friend she could tell anything too,
Did she say that so I could tell her all my business,
or is she a true friend for real or what?

I am constantly reminded
that I will always have a friend in the God I serve.
He is the only friend that I can tell any and all my business to.
He is the only One who will totally understand
whatever I may be going through.
He is the man that will bring you to it and get you through it.
The only One that can and will not forsake you.
So, when you need a friend,
call on HIM!

37

Signs Of Love

Hands full of caress,

your style of dress.

Your lips touch mine,

tingle trickling down my spine.

Full grown, strong, handsome man,

looking at you got me thinking, baby!

You always leave me feeling like I'm the one,

even better, you take me as I am.

The magnetic force of your baritone voice

drew me closer to you as my chakras aligned.

Kim Mattear

Swag in your walk

postured up back as strong as steel.

Beautiful smiles that glow

all over your face blushing simultaneously.

Pop bellies connecting like art heart-to-heart,

eye-to-eye words sounding like a lullaby.

Traffic running smooth this way;

signals that you have the green light.

No need for speed,

merge into the yielding sunflower fields of love.

The stop sign goes up

telling him to pause.

Stop sign goes down

indicating it's okay to proceed now.

MY POEMS OF VIEW

Emergency signals

guarantee no warning when nature's calling.

Clear all emergency exits and detours on all roads,

not even a roadblock can stop this.

There are no dead ends on the roads ahead

our love in which it runs on.

We're on lover's lane drive,

riding our own wave on the journey of love's adventure.

As we step into the name of love

with open arms filled with passionate hugs.

Thoughts of love with nobody else but you,

I am willing to spend the rest of my life with.

For as long as we are together,

our together is our lifetime of forevers.

38

Slipping Away

Most things in life are at our fingertips and within arm's reach.

Get a grip on life or it will get a grip on me.

Arms open wide always ready to receive as I give freely.

The good things in life are free,

free to be me standing tall like a tree.

Being watchful of the slippery leaves crept underneath my feet.

Keeping the grass cut low,

being mindful of the snakes that slither through.

Hissing and kissing, tugging away at you,

steering clear of what's meant to blind you.

Hindrance steady trying

to hold you down while you find strength to climb.

The latter is sturdy, fear had me in a hurry, folks doing me dirty.

Strangers giving me the love that I should receive from family.

Sharing love for their family, out on any limb.

Unconditional and conditional love is no equal.

The one looking down on you

MY POEMS OF VIEW

and talking bad about you, be your own people.

Held on as best as you could, wanting to believe it's all good.

Soon as you step into the room,

voices go mute as all eyes began to stare at you.

No greets, but peep, I keep my head up high,

as no one acknowledges me.

I peep things they don't think I see cause I'm in tuned spiritually.

My vision allows me to see

things going on in places not having to be.

I'm determined to stand my ground

to keep sanity from slipping away from me.

God created the grounds I walk on;

my journey is different from yours.

The path He set for me; my life is a tour to be explored.

Live it up, your life is your life to live, live yours.

My life is mine to live, no mistakes, lead to waste.

No support from loved ones couldn't ever stop my faith.

All this fake love, I can no longer take, I'm slipping away.

I love hard. I refuse to fake love or pretend. I can't take that.

Take nothing in life for granted,

for it will slowly but surely slip away.

Be careful what you ask for, for it will soon be granted one day!

Kim Mattear

39

The Good

Ole Days

The good ole days,

where have they gone?

The fight folded

then the guns let loose more than Tupac in Juice.

Praying for the babies

as they go off to school.

I know they don't belong to me;

they belong to you.

What happens on earth,

is already wrote and blamed on you.

MY POEMS OF VIEW

On another note,

murder was the case that they gave him.

So tired of my brothers

killing one another backwards and forth.

Adding to the numbers, not just our brothers,

our sisters who carry the babies too,

Are being gunned down by our own

as well as government officials.

You see Lord,

what we keep having to go through.

I give all my battles to you Lord,

yes I do.

The good news dwells in You,

so I will continue to look to You.

Joy comes in morning; good days are here;

pray they are here to stay.

Better days lie ahead,

how many more years of this must we take?

Now we're dealing with covid,

right before our eyes, steady playing with our lives.

No weapon formed shall prosper against us as we continue to lean on your understanding God.

Seeking the good out of the bad,

constantly reminds us of your love we have.

Kim Mattear

Good ole days are here to stay;

life is what we make it.

Take the good with the bad,

take none of it for granted.

Enjoy every moment of the day,

for we are equipped.

Gifted in numerous ways,

utilize and you will find one than more of many ways.

There are treasures in life

that you've always wished for.

Good ole days are here,

be brave, have no fear.

What you've wished for is more

than likely near and dear.

Your life depends on it,

search no more and let your soul glow.

Your job is to be you

and who you were born to be.

You will feel happiness, peace,

joy becomes of you.

Good ole days are here,

times have changed, but God's love remains the same.

…

40

The Right Attitude

It takes the right attitude to set a good mood.

Your day can literally go from rough to smooth.

Most times, it all depends on you!

Your attitude defines you; you are your attitude.

Your attitude is you; it determines your day.

Your attitude can be ugly, sometimes they might say it's cute.

There's truth to that, I get that sometimes too.

I'm not perfect, and you know the same thing goes for you.

We're all human, but there's just some things you just don't do.

The best reminder I know in life I say is to pray.

Pray when you wake, pray before you lay, thank Him every day.

Get emotional about Him, forget about them toxins.

A healthy mind applied gets good results all in the right time frame.

Kim Mattear

It's okay to get mad or sad sometimes but,

joy and happiness find its way back again.

Have an awesome day after you determine how good it's gon' get.

Your attitude is what makes you unique more than just your physique.

Speak well, wish well, your attitude reveals how you feel.

Whether it's about you, me, anybody, or anything…

Attitudes are expressed verbally and at times more, physically.

An attitude that stays intact, may be discipline in keeping on his hat.

An attitude that indulges in flips may have to watch their back.

Your attitude is how you dress, finesse and carry yourself.

The way you strut, walk, and talk says a lot about your attitude.

An important factor to people on the outside looking in.

Sometimes that's not a factor neither here nor there.

Your attitude can sometimes come with a stare that holds a glare.

Your attitude says a whole lot just by the way you stroke your hair.

Great attitudes make big bucks, don't get down on your luck!

41

Time Frames

Time has a mind of its own that tic to every tok.
Skip to every minute, tic-tok to the top of the hour.
To top it off it waits for no one; time is always on the run.
The choices and the risk you take, is all the difference a day makes.
What happens today can and will determine your tomorrow.

Betty Wright said it best,
a whole lot of pleasure brings a whole lot of pain.
Janet Jackson told you how time flies when having fun.
What's love got to do with it? Tina Turner had to ask.
That's the way love goes.

Kim Mattear

Time will forever be present

respect its past and the facts of its essence.

Time is patient when you realize it's meaningful virtue.

Time will rush you when you're unprepared for the making.

Time will have you in a hurry leaving you confused.

Time will fly by so fast leaving you mind boggled about what to do next.

Time will be on your side if you do right by it or caught by the lucks of it.

Allowing time to pass you by may cause you to have fits.

Time has a way of finding us and placing us in situations.

Time shows us that no matter where we may go, we still must face it.

Time is a focus factor,

respect the hands of time and pay close attention.

Time has a place for everyone and everything to be said and done.

Time you can trust but you can't trust

everybody with your time.

Time of seasons either passes you by,

are there for a reason, or there for a lifetime.

Time is sweet, not yet simple, but not so hard at all to figure out.

Like people, we make things difficult most of the time.

We could simply save time if we just stop to think before we act.

MY POEMS OF VIEW

Ignoring the warnings signs, carrying on like it means nothing.

Ignoring what time may be revealing before it gets too real!

Make time to check self before checking someone else.

Is time on your side?

Time can be your best friend,

it's possible to borrow, but it just won't wait!

42

Who Has the Power?

It's obvious who got the power.

For whatever reasons it's not totally acknowledged!

There's power in the people,

they don't care to acknowledge that either.

Going in one ear and out the other,

turning cheeks like changing cleats.

Constantly treating the poor bad and the rich so sweet.

Rain down my tears, sun don't watch me weep.

Shine light on me moonshine, put me to sleep.

No sounds from the television brainwashing me.

Waves from the ocean washing over me.

As sirens ride pass with a sister or brother in the back seat.

MY POEMS OF VIEW

Yellow tape roped off all corners, hearing a mother's pain screech.

We stand stronger together than me standing alone.

We're our own worst enemy, can't keep blaming society.

It's only as good as it gets, get it while the getting is good.

There's good in everything, everything is not always good.

God is always good all the time and all the time God is always good.

He has the power to control all things bearing man as witness.

His witness believes in the seen and unseen cause he too has seen.

Fear nothing but God,

for the unknown and unseen can be difficult to see.

God is love; love is the power; He has the power to change all things.

He who has the power is in control of all things.

43
Who Said?

Who said they were better than me?
Who said that I will not be the things in life
I would like to be?
Who said that I will not make it in life?
Who said that I will not marry
and become a good wife?
Who said that I have no education?
Who said that I have no experience
that would get me a good occupation?
Who said that I am mean and stubborn?
Who said that I do not
take good care of my child?
Who said there is no future for me?

MY POEMS OF VIEW

Who said I was a
backstabbing friend?
Who said life is not to cherish?
Who said that black people
are a threat to society?
Who said that I am not black and proud to be?
Who said that we are
against the variety?
Who said we are not dominant over all?
Who said! He said!
She said! They all said!
In this life,
you are not to worry about what people say about you.
Do not stoop low to another one's level for it defines them.
Misery loves company,
if allowed, you will be miserable too!

44

Wish I Had ~~of~~ KNOWN

I wish I had of known
you would have to
go so soon to leave us.

Sunrise in October
for December's sunset
five days before Christmas.

It resonated,
God leaves the bad and takes the good,
funny how life works.

MY POEMS OF VIEW

I wish I had of known.
Do you know how
bad it still hurts?

I feel bad I did not make changes I know I should have...
The secret you held from us
for 13 long years strong.

If I had of known,
change would have
immediately come.

Remembering your immaculate scent,
you would leave behind
on your way to work.

I really miss
helping you tighten up your tie and
buttoning up your shirt.

Your smile
and handsome face lit up the place
standing tall picture perfect.

Always so happy
to see you exclaiming,

Kim Mattear

"That's my Daddy!"

Many tears would fill the room
with so much love for you
came to say farewell.

All they could say is,
"He was truly a good man."
It wasn't hard to tell.

Foot stomping,
smacking of the teeth,
bald up fist in the midst.

Grit faced with disbelief, like the pain of a toothache,
headache, pain tugging war at my soul
and me not wanting to let go.

You are so loved
and tremendously missed
the memories I will not forget.

Wishing you
could be here to see
me live out my dreams.

MY POEMS OF VIEW

Guess I thought I knew
 you would always be
 here with me.

I continue to pray,
think of you
and speak your name every day.

I love and miss you so much Daddy,
it's not always easy
trying to hide this pain.
Fuck cancer!

45

Who's to Blame

We've come a long way compared to
what it was like back in the day.
Don't believe we are the minority;
we are the majority.
Bless this world people
For we are the ones who live in it.
How long will we go on pointing the finger,
blaming others for what they did?
It is okay to forgive,
forgive not, forget not.
Difficulties are sure to come,
though do not have to linger.
Be grateful for our ancestor's
bloodshed poured and spilled before us.
The gruesomeness of black times
thought to have passed by
still exist right before our own eyes.
You are the blame for your own actions,
no matter what happened, then or now.

MY POEMS OF VIEW

Consequences will reap the benefit of those actions,
watch what happen.
For those consequences,
can cough up a lifetime long of dispositions.
No one can read your mind
what you intend to do or speak.
Until your actions show
which side of the link your choice to be,
strong or weak?
Knowledge is power, linked to the
Minds, as to how we choose to think.
No one else is to blame,
let that thought sit to sink.
Blaming others and pointing
fingers blind the eye to see.
Blinded from light causes
behaviors that will not save you,
pray for peace and its stability.
Open your heart for love,
keep an open mind for
like minds and kindred souls.
Our black heroes, leaders, and
educators struggled for a freedom come future.
Leaving legacies behind and
leaving hopes for us to
live for dreams to come alive.

Kim Mattear

How on earth would I know
if it had not been for those
who paved the way for me?
It is important and our responsibility
for our children to be the best that they can be.
Teach them our history,
it's more to it than slavery, victory is one.
We are the blame for what happens to us,
let's make it happen.
We always find a way to make something out of nothing.
We are the history all the fuss is about no mystery,
read to understand His story.

MY POEMS OF VIEW

46

Women Who Love *Too Much*

Women who love too much,
pour out countless amounts of love.

Women who love too much,
give too much of themselves.

Women who love too much,
feel out of touch.

Women who love too much,
expect too much from others.

Kim Mattear

Women who love too much,
can be very vulnerable.

Women who love too much,
do not allow anyone to disrespect you.

Women who love too much,
God will always love you more than man.

Women who love too much,
fall deep when it is only the beginning.

Women who love too much,
know that some beginnings transition into endings.

Women who love too much,
focus on winning.

Women who love too much,
keep your eyes on the prize.

Women who love too much,
you are grand.

Women who love too much,
love no man better than you can love yourself.

MY POEMS OF VIEW

Women who love too much,
excuses are crutches we use when we are confused.

Women who love too much,
have discernment for better terms of endearment.

Women who love too much,
do not ever stop loving, YOU.

Women who love too much,
the right one for you will come soon.

Women who love too much,
when you settle for less, you get less.

Women who love too much,
the best is yet to come.

Women who love too much,
look forward to living your best life is yet to come.

Women who love too much,
God is love and for that you will be blessed.

Women who love too much,
love will be put to the test.

Kim Mattear

Women who love too much,
my love is your love.

Women who love too much,
it gets lonely sometimes.

Women who love too much,
you are not alone.

Women who love too much,
lighten your heavy load.

Women who love too much,
always remember that God is in control.

Women who love too much,
real love is good for the soul.

MY POEMS OF VIEW

47

Women

W - Wombman
O - Overseer
M - Magnifying
E - Epitome
N - Naturistic

Women you stand for more than
what you believe in or even know.

You open your hearts as wide as the
walls of our wombs' pushing babies out.

Your strength carries loads of love,
generosity, sophisticated nurturers.

To say the least,
you are stronger than a beast.

Kim Mattear

Emotional high creatures with
electrifying, defining features.

Allowing life's experiences
to be our best teacher.

The thought of living
without us is impossible.

Your presence says a mouth
full even while in silence.

Women we are stronger
Together than ever standing alone.

When you fall, dust it off and
get back up like a game of hopscotch.

Sometimes the road gets rough,
you are a diamond in the rut.

Your soulmate awaits you for
perfect timing, time needs no rush.

Let no man come between us
for God has one for each of us.

MY POEMS OF VIEW

Let not fear nor anger be
your energy's recipe.

Overcome your fears and fear
nothing but God, cause He got you and me.

He will bless you
when it is your time.

We are in no competition;
we all have a vision state of mind.

No mission is impossible for
any of us to complete.

I am every woman;
it is all in me.

48

You Do What That Man Tells You To?

The one man we should be listening to, we don't listen to enough! Run to Him for rescue, it will always be the best decision one can ever do.

What makes you run back to a man who abuse you emotionally, mentally, or physically? It may take for me to be in your shoes, honestly speaking, it wouldn't be me.

I refuse to allow some dude to do to me the things he does to you. Stand your ground, save yourself, you have to find a way out.

When you escape run fast and don't ever look back.
We serve a jealous God, who is always there even when life gets hard.

MY POEMS OF VIEW

Allow Him to fight your battles, stop blocking your own blessing which will leave you scarred. We must praise Him first, be very careful what man or woman has to say.

Everyone's advice is not always the best advice you're going to receive in life. Nobody's money is that important and my heart is constantly bleeding.

It's time to start believing that your validation does not lie in the hands of heathens'. He's not your husband nor your father and you do anything he tell you to do.

You feel weak, allowing him to lower your self-esteem every chance, it seems. Now that he's caused you to be so blind, it's even harder for you to see.

An abusive man is no stronger than you, for he is also weak and unaware that he is. You only have one life to live, do not live it in fear for he is not the only man that exist.

Fear is a disease trapped in a box unable to find its way out. Don't let that to continue to be you, you are more than beautiful itself.

You're that diamond in a rough, you don't look like what

you've been through. Get out now, chance will find you like being brave is the only choice you ever knew.

Act over your life the same way you've allowed man to have control over you. A man should bring out the best in you, not the worst.

You can do bad all by yourself, two heads are said to be better than one. Scared to be alone, you're not alone, no more being a prisoner in your own home.

That man only does to you what you allow him to say and do. Try using the only man worthy of praising and the one that created you.

MY POEMS OF VIEW

49

You Know What

To Do

Uh-Uh! Y'all better get up,
the party ain't started yet!

Get me a six-pack of "Old English" and
pour it all out for me, "You know what to do!"

Kim Mattear

Do not mourn me, join me,
"You know what to do!"

Play my song! Jam for me,
get your groove on, dance for me.

 You know what!
Only if my husband was here.

Get up!
"You know what to do!"

You know what!
All you slime, slick, and you wicked, son-of-a...

You know what?

You ain't got to go home,
but you gotta get the hell outta of here!

You know what to do!
Now get out!!!

Keep Your Loved Ones Memory Alive!

MY POEMS OF VIEW

ABOUT THE AUTHOR

MY POEMS OF VIEW

Kim Mattear

BORN TO LEROY & CHERRYL Mattear, Kim Mattear was born and raised in Los Angeles, California, where she attended several schools: Arlington Heights Elementary School; Mount Vernon Junior High School (*now known as Johnny Cochran Jr. Middle School*); Dorsey, Crenshaw, and Los Angeles High School, to name a few. To ensure she had a skill under her belt, she attended Los Angeles Trade Technical Community College. She also attended "City College," a private institute located in Fort Lauderdale, Florida while studying Broadcasting. Mattear has a brother and a sister, and she also has one daughter, whom she loves dearly.

Getting into the professional side of life, Mattear owns a music publishing company, *Golden Life Music Publishing* via Broadcast Music Inc. She is the CEO and Founder of "*Be You Apparel Enterprise*," a clothing line, that she owns and operates "Exercise with Herbalife" as a Herbalife Distributor and she's also tapping into Digital Network Market, helping lead the way to financial freedom. Mattear has always loved to write, dance, and skate. She desires to be creative, expressing and utilizing her ideas in ways to reach the world. To top it off, she has a sense of humor out of this world which requires lots of laughter.

In addition to the previously mentioned strengths mentioned above, Mattear's passion for writing has led her to become a future best-selling author signed with SHE PUBLISHING LLC, where she'd build a life-long partnership and launch the sister company "Golden Publishing, LLC." While taking on this new endeavor, Mattear is also working on new music (a new anticipated album). She is an actress, and her sixth movie

MY POEMS OF VIEW

appearance is scheduled to be released late 2021 or early 2022. Be on the lookout for *High Maintenance: 3*.

The release of *My Poems of View* has halted another unique project Mattear has in store. This project is near and dear to her heart. *Project Next L.A.* is her baby, and means a lot to her, so she really wants to take her time with delivering the project. Mattear has anticipated the release of her first poetry book for so long and wasn't sure it would come as soon as it did.

Enduring the loss of both parents within a 5-year period, Mattear is determined to succeed. If her parents were alive, her mom, who was her biggest fan, would say, "*I knew you would do it. You got what it takes. I told you, you're a star!*" Mattear's mom would be so proud. Mattear's dad would also be glad to see her accomplishing her dreams. He truly believed in Mattear and was the first to witness most of her writings from a little girl. He would genuinely say, "*You finally did it, Kimmie!*" Mattear's parents would confess how very proud they are of her, but it doesn't stop there. Mattear's friends would say they're not surprised by her success because she has always been good at writing.

A message from the future best-selling author:
Put passion in everything you do and never give up as this is precisely what I've done and will continue to do!

Kim Mattear

MY POEMS OF VIEW

ACKNOWLEDGMENTS

WHAT'S OLD TO ME is new to you. That saying rings true for me and my first book here. God is the reason for every season, I must say. Not that I even planned to have a book published so soon. Or the fact that it's a book of poetry, the first form of literature I fell in love with. Being that this opportunity came out of nowhere, which tells me that it was nothing but God. God led me to the opportunity, and just like He knew I would, I grasped it. I rarely let opportunities slip away from me if I can help it.

My parents didn't have to sign me up for much of anything. I always took the initiative for myself. That's what my mother adored about me, constantly comparing me to my father regarding my work ethic. She would remind me that I was a hard worker like my father. She was surprised when she saw it in me. It made her smile as she would feel a sense of pride that would also rub off on me. Although

MY POEMS OF VIEW

they're not here with me, I always feel their presence. I speak to them just like they are here, just like I speak to God. God put S.H.E Publishing, and I in the paths of one another as the spirit worked on us a collaboration. A project of mines was sitting on the back burner at the time. I always had a book in mind, but not at the current moment. I was working on music, as well as a collaboration.

In detail, I have an extraordinary project that I call my baby "Project Next L.A." "I Love L.A."! It's a project that I dedicate to Nipsey Hussle, Kobe & Gigi Bryant, the beautiful life, soul, and spirit of "Lyric "Yhung" Chanel," and my dear child- hood friend who also passed away, Che'Kesha Newton (also known as my personal assistant). This book is my baby too. "Project Next L.A." needs all my focus and attention. This book was a must as well. With that being said, I can't be in two places or more at the same time.

Let's just say that because revisiting and revising these poems took me on an emotional rollercoaster ride. I wasn't so sure I was ready for it, but I had to go through it. God brought me to it, so I must go through it. Stop running from the pain, and here I had no choice as bad as I want to put out this book. I couldn't run from the pain. From the first page of poems down to the last page of poems, on different days leading into a different week, I've experienced feelings that have come over me that I can't explain. I fell weak, speechless, joyous each time. I've cried my heart and soul into my pillow, so the walls could not hear, taking me back to the times when my mom and dad were well alive and here. They were my biggest supporters ever to date!

Feel Free to Google Me:
@Kim Mattear and/or Realady
@goldenpublishing.she

SPECIAL THANKS

FIRST AND FOREMOST, I thank God and Jesus Christ for everything. I'm very grateful for His mercy, glory, grace, and favor. I am nothing without God. I thank my Mom and Dad for giving birth to me. I thank them for teaching me to be the best that I can be. I thank them for all they did, and all they would do if they were still here. I give thanks to my third-grade teacher Mr. Drum- mond; it wasn't just what he did. It's what he said. He wrote on my final report card of the 3rd grade, *"I hope to purchase one of your books from the bookstore one day."* To this day, I'm still grateful for his encouragement. It always stayed with me. It never left me.

I thank most of the teachers I had. They would always motivate and inform me of the qualities they'd seen in me. They recognized my good grades and the skills I posse-ssed.

I also thank my daughter, Kimyah Henderson, for giving me a reason to live and leaving her a legacy for generations to learn about and fulfill. I'm also thankful to my little brother, Jason Mattear, for always believing in me and supporting me wherever, whenever, or however he can. I appreciate him for that! I thank my Godmother, Shirley Colquitt, for believing in me as well. She was another cheerleader, along with my Mom. I thank Lady Dice (C. Nicole Jackson) for being my support team in everything I do since becoming business partners with her. I've learned a lot from her in progressing in various industries of women in entrepreneurship pushing to break barriers.

I would also like to thank my childhood friend, my best friend Gesele Muhummad, for her everlasting support throughout the years, allowing me the peace in the right place to be, which made it possible for me to see this opportunity in the first place before my eyes. Finally, I give a warm thanks to Shenitha and the entire S.H.E. Publishing Team. I feel this experience was meant to be. I must personally thank Queen Shenitha for her welcoming me with open arms and extending more than just a service to me. I appreciate and thank her for her consideration and the tremendous amount of moral support she continuously offers. I thank any and everyone who has ever believed in me and continues to believe in me. I thank God for everything overall.